Reflections from Hell

Richard Lewis'
GUIDE ON HOW NOT TO LIVE

IMAGES BY
Carl Nicholas Titolo

FOREWORD BY
Larry David

PREFACE BY
Christopher Murray

 **powerHouse Books**

BROOKLYN, NEW YORK

TO MY WONDROUS WIFE, JOYCE.
Richard

To Angela... Amore grande sempre.
Carl

INTRODUCTION FROM HELL
Richard Lewis

Over four decades ago, fresh out of the Ohio State University with a B.S. in Business (although still managing through the years to get screwed by thousands of managers, promoters, and agents) and as broke as I ever thought I could be, from day one I only felt relief by jotting down dark, comedic premises, with the dream of one day expounding upon them and becoming a stand-up comedian. I'm still writing down these premises whenever they strike me as funny and honest and I have hundreds of thousands of them on file. Somehow, these thoughts enabled me to finally pay the bills as a comedian and turn what was initially a seemingly psychotic show business fantasy into a career that is still going strong and fueled by similar jokes and reflections to those in this book—thoughts which on paper still sound as hopeless and insane as I felt when I dreamt I could make a living as a humorist.

In the mid-eighties when I was introduced to the art of Carl Nicholas Titolo I was blown to smithereens. A year ago, after having become somewhat of a patron of Carl's work, I had some sort of epiphany. As I loved his astounding imagery, and knowing he dug my words, I asked him if he'd be up to take some of my insanity and fill in the reflections with his own extraordinary insanity.

It took him a moment to say yes and here it is. Hopefully this is only Volume One as I have a bottomless pit of my doomsday reflections that Mr. Titolo is only ecstatic to illustrate to shed some light on my darkness. I recommend that children stay far away from these words and images unless you are cocksure they are able to discern the difference between pure jokes and honest-to-goodness fear.

I am blessed to have Carl visually fill in the holes of this first set of reflections. Be my guest and hit your knees and recite these every morning before you start your day, get a huge laugh from the illustrations, and, if you don't mind, pray for my well-being. Mostly though, please laugh and know that you are way ahead of the game not being me.

I warned you.

THE ARTIST ON THE COMEDIAN

Carl Nicholas Titolo

For almost three decades I have been fortunate to have Richard Lewis as a friend, an inspiration, and a patron. Though our traveling time is reflected in different forms our overlaps are many. Listening, reading, and watching Richard Lewis on stage is like being in the blender of his brain on high speed, he stops and starts where others rarely travel. He can make you smile at the mention of death's door, and bring tears to your eyes on a riff about an egg. For an image-maker the collaboration is a dream, an opportunity to put a visual flame to his narrative flint. He speeds on a roller coaster one moment and floats in the comfort of a womb the next. This perpetual changing of the radio station moves like an impromptu jazz session with little or no warning as to what emotional key will be next. A stream of consciousness, an order in chaos, taking one on a journey to unexpected places in one's heart and mind. To be a passenger, an invitation to interpret his supersonic observations is to an image-maker what the opportunity for a musician would be to play all the instruments in an orchestra. A diverse visual sound track of inner thoughts. Regardless of his subject, what Richard possesses is the ability to make one think, not only about how what he says affects him, but also how it relates to those who are fortunate enough to share his inner thoughts and observations. He pauses and accelerates when you least expect it. But no matter his speed, he makes you think and these days we all need an inspiring conjurer. From literal narrative images to conceptual visual reductions, his words, his thoughts, his essence are the creative sparks entering my head and exiting my hand. Come and share the ride.

Thank you Richard.

FOREWORD
Larry David

Here's a good piece of advice: If you should ever have the misfortune of crossing paths with Richard Lewis, do not—I repeat—DO NOT give him your personal information. No address, phone number, email—especially email. Nothing! If he asks you for it (and he will) and you can't think of a quick excuse, just say no, you'd rather not. Be prepared, though—he'll be hurt. He'll tell you he's devastated. He loves that word. He uses it a lot. That's how he got me to write this. He asked me, I turned him down, and he told me he was devastated. In a moment of weakness, I caved. So stay strong. Don't succumb. Because if you do, your life will never be the same.

You'll wake up every morning to a barrage of emails. It's actually the closest thing to spam that's not spam. You'll get constant updates as to what he's doing and with whom he's doing it. Press clippings, reviews, Tweets, aphorisms, and ruminations on his life and death. And what you perceive to be private emails have actually been copied to fifty other people. All in all, you'll begin to dread that little bell going off on your phone. You will conveniently forget to charge it and start leaving it at home.

There are also calls—lots of them. Within a week or two, mark my words, he will turn you into a screener. He knows this, which is why he changed to "Unknown Number." Well, it's not unknown anymore. It's him. If you don't take the call—and I urge you not to—he will then leave a message, which will be so long that he will invariably get cut off, at which point he will call you back and very likely get cut off again. Soon your voicemail box will be filled up and you won't be able to get any messages, even important ones. Knowing him could cost you a job, a relationship, and quite possibly your life.

Many of these messages will be him badgering you to get together. When you finally give in—and very few humans can resist the onslaught—you will receive another bombardment of calls and emails, reminding you of date, time, and place. You'll assure him you've already confirmed this multiple times, and then a few hours later...voilà!

When you do finally meet, a few things will become apparent during your encounter. First is his excessive use of the word "shrink," which he uses as often as teens use the word "like." It's almost a tic. It will also dawn on you, perhaps during dessert, that you haven't uttered a word. Maybe a few "uh-huhs," but that's it. And make sure to get extra napkins because he'll be using yours to write down new jokes, which occur with an almost alarming rapidity. Often you will notice he'll be staring at you with an odd look, until you realize he isn't really looking at you, but at his reflection in the window behind you. You and all you possess, especially your clothing, will be mocked relentlessly and unmercifully, and when he leaves, you will be exhausted and will want to go right to bed. You will not be able to read or even watch television. I might add that you will also laugh. Possibly harder than you've ever laughed before. You will be in awe of how his synapses fire, how he observes life around him, how his brain sorts and compiles all the images it takes in. You might also notice how kind and sweet and generous he is.

Carl Nicholas Titolo, who did the illustrations for this book, is a prime example of that generosity. Carl is a painter of prodigious gifts and has such an authentic presence that when I'm around him I feel even phonier than I normally do. Because he couldn't afford a loft, he was consigned to painting on tiny canvases in a tiny eastside apartment that he shared with his beautiful wife, Angela. Enter Richard Lewis, who volunteered to pay the rent on a loft for him. I am now the proud owner of three Titolos, which were done in that space. Unfortunately, no one ever comes to my house, so I'm the only one who gets to see them, although recently the UPS guy did catch a glimpse of one and went on and on about it until I had to practically push him out the door.

Lewis and Titolo have much in common. First and foremost, each is obsessed with and completely devoted to their work. They are both original, prolific, and incorruptible. And if that's not enough, Titolo goes through even more napkins than Lewis, drawing everything from saltshakers to the unsuspecting mark sitting across from him. So if you plan on meeting up with Titolo, be sure to check yourself out in the mirror beforehand. As with Lewis, he sees all, and that picture could very well wind up in a museum.

This book is a marriage of artist and comedian. I'm usually skeptical about marriages of any kind, but this one works.

PREFACE
Chris Murray

*Deep into that darkness peering, long I stood there wonder-
ing,*

   fearing...

—*The Raven*, Edgar Allan Poe

Not long ago on a cold winter day in New York City I went
for a visit to the Morgan Library and Museum to see an exhibition on Edgar Allan Poe called *Terror of the Soul*. On display were
handwritten manuscripts by Poe, first editions of his books, vin-
tage photographs and paintings, tributes from other renowned
writers, among them Oscar Wilde, Charles Dickens, Vladimir
Nabokov, and Terry Southern, as well as numerous other remark-
able artifacts and documents from the life of Poe.

There was, however, one item that I kept returning to
that fascinated me. It was an illustrated edition of Poe's most famous poem, *The Raven*, translated into French by the symbolist
Stéphane Mallarmé and published as *Le Corbeau* in 1875. The artist for this stunning edition was none other than the great French
painter Édouard Manet. Manet's dark and brooding lithographs
fit perfectly the mood and narrative of the poem that had made
Poe something of a celebrity.

While enjoying the combination of Poe's words and
Manet's art I could not help but draw a comparison to the words
of Richard Lewis and the images of Carl Nicholas Titolo as seen
in *Reflections from Hell*. Just a few weeks before going to the Poe
exhibition I had the opportunity to see the original art that
Titolo had spent over a year creating for Lewis' humorous and
compelling words...his reflections.

I won't soon forget seeing Lewis' words combined with Titolo's works on paper. The collaboration immediately engaged me in a way that was intimate and personal while at the same time existential and universal. Their work together is a contemporary personification of creative angst from which we can laugh at the dilemmas of life we all face.

Like Poe, Lewis deals with the darker side of life. They both are storytellers who defy convention. Lewis is famous for his humor while Poe is known for his horror. Yet humor and horror are not so different. They both can reveal our fears as well as our dreams.

That Richard Lewis is a comedic genius there is no doubt. Carl Nicholas Titolo's images are not only artfully created, they are clever and sophisticated. With their creative energy as our guide we take this journey, as Dante into the Inferno, to the world of Richard Lewis' words and Carl Nicholas Titolo's art.

Reflections from Hell

I'm cautiously
optimistic.

My mother tried to
switch me at birth.

Today I made the worst
of a great situation.

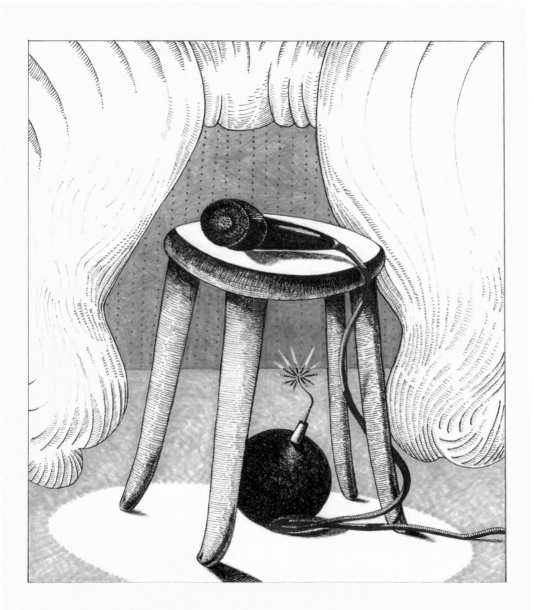

Happiness
is overrated.

I'm thinking of hiring
assistants to vent for me.

The pesticides for my family tree obviously failed.

Fortunately for me,
most of my exes'
orgasms happened
with me out of the room.

If you feel ill
at ease in your own skin
get it tailored.

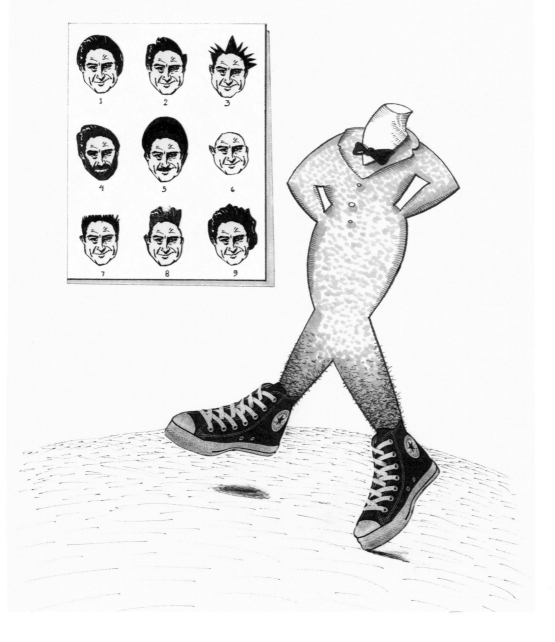

Nothing makes sense
when I try
to figure it out.

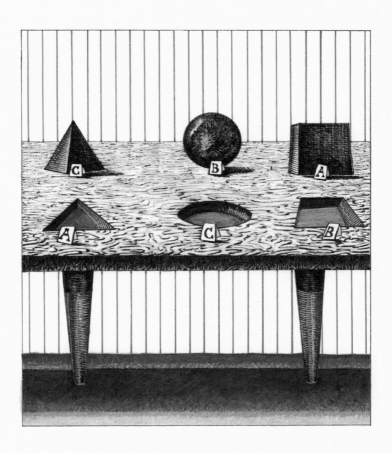

I used to think that tropical depressions were my relatives in Florida.

I used Viagra once
and got a four hour
cowlick.

I burn calories by
worrying in place.

My shrink is so burned
from our sessions
she now blames her
own childhood on me.

I've been to the
mountaintop and got
bit by red ants.

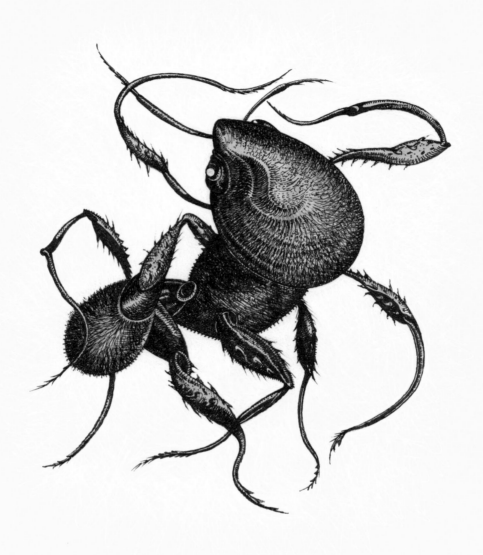

My parents didn't want
to get a divorce
until they passed away.

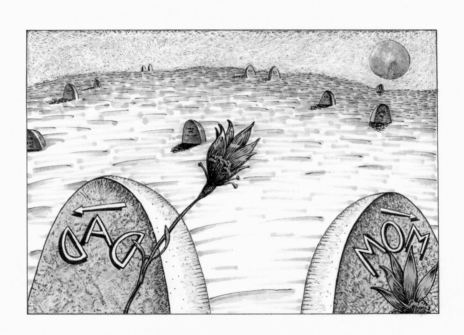

Sadly, I was thrown off the Jewish center track team by a parochial school that claimed my sneakers gave me an unfair advantage.

What a shame that love
is a two-way street.

I dreamt I was
reincarnated and
came back as myself.

My wife loves me for
what I could've been.

I'm solid as long as I keep a distance from myself.

I've always had a tough time telling a woman that I loved her directly.

After I was born,
my mother asked friends
to breast-feed me.

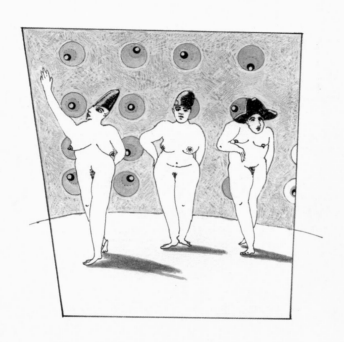

The best sparring partner I can have is myself.

I'm so isolated that
most of the time
I don't know where I am.

I'm trying to drop an asshole a day from my life, and doing the math, I'll be done in the year 3011.

There's nothing to fear
but life itself.

I slept all day and
didn't get any sleep.

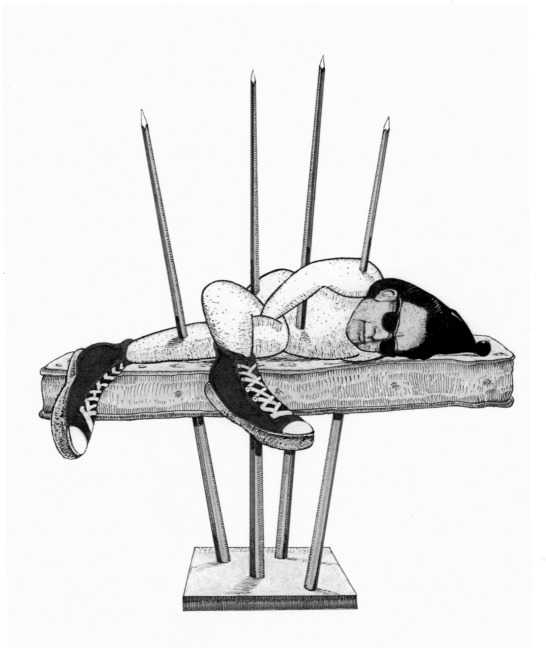

Bring your own meds week...

Trust me,
hanging on to
resentments merely
empowers jerk-offs.
Once I stop
resenting myself I'm
home free.

Failing
is
overrated.

The
monkey on my back
is me.

My nightmares have coming attractions.

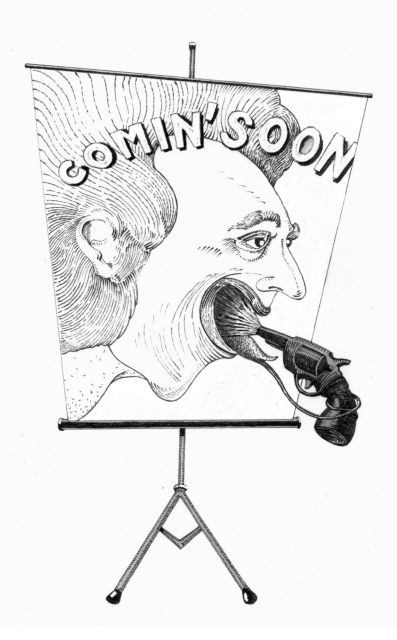

The morning my shrink
asked me to lighten up.

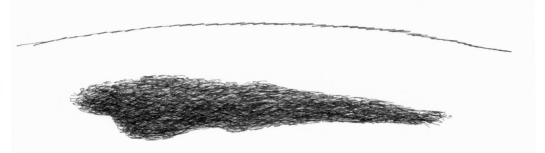

Mirror mirror
on the wall,
who's the happiest
of them all?

I wanted
to drown
in the womb.

My mother
always drove me in
reverse so I would get
the wrong impression.

The best way to go to couple's counseling is alone.

I'm so paranoid, I hack my own computer.

The only positive
memory I have about
my blackouts
was that I was
never depressed.

I pick more fights with myself than with anyone else.

My favorite
habit is thinking that I
can play God.

Desperation is my
sweet spot.

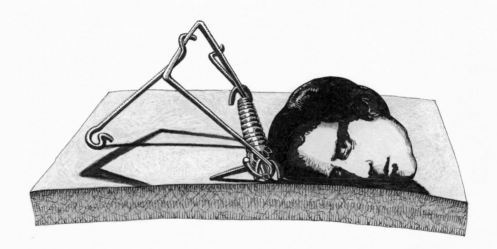

I always know
something's
terribly wrong but I
can't put my finger on it.

I don't care what anyone tells you; watch your back.

The worst
audience I ever had
were my parents.

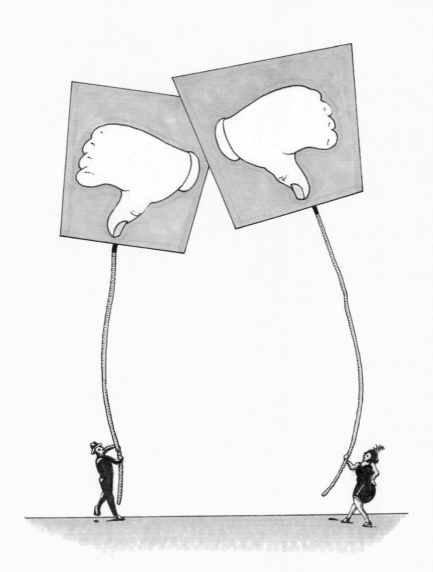

A fan just sent me a "don't get well" card.

I was born with a silver spoon in my nose.

Lying is a matter of perception.

The longer I live the more I have to worry.

Relax,
I'll take the hit for
everyone's misery.

Acknowledgements

First, I acknowledge myself for my good fortune in meeting Mr. Titolo through my oldest friend, Jon Dembrow. I instantly was wild over Carl's style of painting, which to me was reminiscent of Max Ernst, Mel Brooks, and how my brain works.

This collaboration is a dream come true, albeit in a nightmarish fashion. For my true friends who accept me and my favorite flaws and those who handle my career, I can only say to you, thank God I'm not crazier. To my longtime spokeswoman and publicist, Michelle Marx, someone who courageously has tolerated my eccentricities and worked around them to tell the world of any alleged talents of mine, she has been miraculous.

Of course, this couldn't have happened without my friendship with the wildly passionate Chris Murray, the legendary author, editor, writer, curator, and art dealer. He is a man who devoted a lifetime, with his extraordinary love and hard work, to making magic by helping artists' and photographers' projects become more than a pipe dream. He is unlike anyone I've ever met who occasionally wears a suit. How could I ever curb my enthusiasm for Larry David, a true genius and pal, who was born in the same hospital as I was three days later, yet already with a half-written script clutched in his tiny hands. Knowing our relationship, he instantly started mocking my rosy cheeks but all is forgiven as he honored us with his David-esque Foreword. Almost last but not least, I'm eternally grateful to the groundbreaking, hip publishers at powerHouse Books and all those they leaned on to make *Reflections from Hell* a reality. Finally, the forty-five years of fans who have dug me, by understanding my thin line between narcissism and self-deprecating humor—I truly owe you my career.

Richard Lewis

The mere mention of the word collaboration always made my heart skip a beat for I have always worked in my studio alone, in solitude, without consideration of outside opinions. This book project changed my perception and resulted in a magical journey, working with an exceptional group of individuals at powerHouse Books. Craig Cohen, Will Luckman, and the supporting crew made this project as smooth as butter in a hot, cast-iron pan. Chris Murray, a thoughtful, spiritual guide throughout the entire process, acted as the creative ringmaster, coordinating the participants making sure we all not only understood our specific expertise but produced our best work without comprising our integrity. I would also like to acknowledge the amazing design of the book by Gustaf Torling. He clearly understood our intent to capture the true essence of Richard Lewis, a great performer's life onstage.

Thank you all,
Carl Nicholas Titolo

REFLECTIONS FROM HELL:
RICHARD LEWIS' GUIDE ON HOW NOT TO LIVE

Text © 2015 Richard Lewis
Illustration © 2015 Carl Nicholas Titolo
Foreword © 2015 Larry David
Preface © 2015 Chris Murray

Art Direction by Gustaf Törling
www.torling.com

Published in the United States by powerHouse Books,
a division of powerHouse Cultural Entertainment, Inc.
37 Main Street, Brooklyn, NY 11201-1021
telephone 212.604.9074, fax 212.366.5247
e-mail: info@powerHouseBooks.com
website: www.powerHouseBooks.com

First edition, 2015

Library of Congress Control Number: 2014959151

ISBN 978-1-57687-745-6

Printed and bound through Asia Pacific Offset

10 9 8 7 6 5 4 3 2 1

Printed and bound in China